Martial Ar

Quotes, Maxims, & Sto.

M000094618

To: Robert,
Congratulations on your
black belt! With best
wishes from Diana, Ashley,
and Eric.

Martial Arts Wisdom
Quotes, Maxims, & Stories for the Martial Artist

Bohdi Sanders, Ph.D.

Copyright © 2014 by Bohdi Sanders, Ph.D.

Library of Congress Cataloging-in-Publication Data
Bohdi Sanders, 1962-
title

ISBN – 978-1-937884-09-3

1. Martial Arts. 2. Self-Help. 3. Philosophy.

Kaizen Quest Publishing

Acknowledgments

I want to express my sincere appreciation to my beautiful wife, Tracey, for all of her patience for my many hours spent at my computer researching and compiling *Martial Arts Wisdom*. Without her love and support this book would have never come to fruition. I also want to thank her for taking time out from her busy schedule to read and edit *Martial Arts Wisdom*. That is just one of the perks of being married to a great English teacher.

In addition, I want to thank all of my readers who continue to buy my books and pursue the warrior lifestyle. All of your emails and letters definitely let me know that my books and writing are making a difference in the world. So many of you ask where I find all the quotes that I use in my writing, now you have them at your fingertips, well, a lot of them anyway. Enjoy!

Table of Contents

Introduction

Martial Arts Wisdom is a quote book for the martial artist and the warrior. It is filled with over 800 quotes, maxims, and stories, all designed to provide the martial artist, the warrior, the law enforcement officer, and the military men and women with wisdom to help guide them on their path.

I have intentionally not organized the quotes, maxims, and stories in *Martial Arts Wisdom* into different categories. Instead, I tried to include an eclectic mix on each page. This basically allows the reader to open to any page and get a variety of wisdom. It also allows *Martial Arts Wisdom* to be used in a manner similar to the *I-Ching*, where the reader can mentally focus on a question, and then open to a specific page and see how the wisdom from that page applies to the question.

I have, however, included an extensive index for the reader's convenience. The authors are listed just as they appear under each quote, most by first name first. For example, if you wanted to look up quotes by William James, you would look under "W" and not under "J." I have also included subject matter in the index, so the reader may look up all quotes pertaining to certain subjects.

Also, I have not included any commentary on the quotes or maxims. The purpose of *Martial Arts Wisdom* is for the martial artist or the warrior to reflect on the specific quotes and stories, and to come to their own conclusion as to how the wisdom contained applies to their own life. I have other books where I explain my philosophy on the warrior lifestyle and martial arts and warrior philosophy. This specific book is meant for the reader to quietly reflect on the wisdom for himself or herself.

The reader will also find that he or she recognizes the authors of many of the quotes, as being martial arts masters or famous martial artists. But, many of the other quotes are not by martial artists. Do not simply disregard the quotes by those authors who are not martial artists. Every quote, maxim, and story included in *Martial Arts Wisdom*, is included because of its value to the martial artist and the warrior. If at first, you don't see the value in a specific quote, spend some time reflecting on it and the meaning of each quote will come to you.

In addition, please read each quote with an open mind. Reflect on the wisdom of what is being said, more than on who the author of the quote may be. I take wisdom wherever I may find it and apply it to the warrior lifestyle. Some of the authors included in this compilation may not be who you would expect to find in a book designed to impart wisdom, but I assure you, if you read each quote, maxim, and story with an open mind, you will find that each has its own value.

If you disregard a quote because the author is not historically respected, you will miss out. Remember that history is many times written by those with their own agendas. Wisdom comes in many different forms and from people and places you may not expect. You can learn something from everyone, if you allow yourself to do so.

Lastly, *Martial Arts Wisdom* is not meant to be read straight through and then set aside. Take your time and refer back to the wisdom contained in this book over and over again. Meditate on it and integrate it into your life. Make it a part of who you are. If you do this, I can assure you that you will find that *Martial Arts Wisdom* will be well worth your time.

The wisdom within will change your outlook regarding certain beliefs, and will solidify other beliefs that you already have. Take your time and enjoy your journey through the wisdom that has been given to us from the masters of peace, war, martial arts, the warrior lifestyle, and life. The amount of wisdom in *Martial Arts Wisdom* is tremendous.

I hope that you thoroughly enjoy the wisdom that I have compiled for you. Make sure not to merely read it, but to also apply it to your life. You can read all the wisdom in the world, but it won't help you any if you don't apply it to your life. Incorporate the philosophy of the warrior lifestyle in your life and you will find that your life will be more balanced. And, you will be more prepared to handle whatever may come your way. Enjoy!

Bohdi Sanders

Martial Arts Wisdom
Quotes, Maxims, & Stories for the Martial Artist

Bohdi Sanders, Ph.D.

The student must become a true warrior
in an age where there are no more warriors.
Kensho Furuya

One must make the warrior walk
his everyday walk.
Miyamoto Musashi

Do not be tricked into thinking that there are
no crocodiles just because the water is still.
Malaysian Proverb

He is victorious who knows
when and when not to fight.
Sun Tzu

All opponents have two arms, two legs,
and can be beaten, just like yourself.
Matsura Seizan

Always make certain that you are in
a better position than your enemy.
Takuan Soho

You should be calm outside,
but keep your mind alert and prepared.
Yagyu Tajimanokami Munenori

When irate, clear-minded men never
show it then and there. Holding it in,
they watch for an opportune moment.
Tiruvalluvar

The ordinary man is involved in action,
the hero acts. An immense difference.
Henry Miller

Civilize the mind,
but make savage the body.
Mao Zedong

Progress comes to those who train and train.
Reliance on secret techniques will get you nowhere.
Morihei Ueshiba

Virtue, integrity and courage are my priorities.
I can be approached, but never pushed;
befriended but never coerced;
killed but never shamed.
Yi Sunshin

The man who is secure within himself
has no need to prove anything with force,
so he can walk away from a fight with dignity and
pride. He is the true martial artist – a man so strong
inside that he has no need to demonstrate his power.
Ed Parker

One mind, any weapon.
Hunter B. Armstrong

An able man shows his spirit by
gentle words and resolute actions;
he is neither hot nor timid.
Philip Dormer Stanhope

Opportunities multiply as they are seized.
Sun Tzu

Warriors are not what you think of as warriors.
The warrior is not someone who fights... The warrior,
for us, is one who sacrifices himself for the good of others.
His task is to take care of the elderly, the defenseless,
those who cannot provide for themselves, and
above all, the children, the future of humanity.
Sitting Bull

First see to it that you, yourself, are all right,
then think of defeating an opponent.
The Way of the Spear

Even when called out by a single foe, remain on guard,
for you are always surrounded by a host of enemies.
Morihei Ueshiba

The ultimate aim of karate lies not in victory or defeat
but in the perfection of the character of its participants.
Gichin Funakoshi

The man of true valor lies between the
extremes of cowardice and of rashness.
Miguel de Cervantes

Behavior influences consciousness.
Right behavior means right consciousness...
The actions of every instant, every day, must be right...
Every gesture is important.
Taisen Deshimaru

In seeking to save another,
beware of drowning yourself.
Sir Francis Osborne

The focused mind can pierce through stone.
Japanese Maxim

By keeping your weapons in order,
your enemy will be subjugated.
Nagarjuna

Never get angry except on purpose.
Japanese Maxim

There are people in every era who,
however adverse the environment, are
not corrupted, do not become degenerate.
Masaaki Hatsumi

He who fears being conquered is sure of defeat.
Napoleon Bonaparte

Strength is defeated by strategy.
Philippine Proverb

The only reason a warrior fights is to win.
Miyamoto Musashi

Peace is not the lack of war,
but an inner virtue which has its
source in the courage of the soul.
Baruch Spinoza

If you believe, then you have already taken
the first step towards your achievement.
Rickson Gracie

Avoiding danger is not cowardice.
Philippine Proverb

The important thing is to be always
moving forward, little by little.
Masutatsu Oyama

Think, feel, and act like a warrior.
Set yourself apart from the rest of
society by your personal excellence.
Forrest E. Morgan

The way is in training.
Miyamoto Musashi

Control the situation in such a way
that nobody knows how you control it.
Vladimir Vasiliev

If you are patient in a moment of anger,
you will escape a hundred days of sorrow.
Chinese Proverb

Avoid instead of containing.
Contain instead of damaging.
Damage instead of mutilating.
Mutilate instead of killing.
Gichin Funakoshi

Maybe, Maybe Not

During the Warring States period in China, a farmer lived with his only son, with whom he depended on to help do the farm work. They had only one horse, which they loved, and which was vital to help with their farming.

One day the horse ran away and the farmer complained to the village elder that he didn't know how he was going to survive without his trusted horse. "What terrible luck this is," he exclaimed.

The elder replied, "Maybe, maybe not. We will see."

This angered the farmer, but he held his tongue and returned home, thinking the elder must be losing his senses.

A few days later, the farmer's horse returned, leading a wild mare back to the farm. The farmer was delighted at his good luck, and exclaimed to the village elder, "My luck has changed! What a blessing this is!"

Again, the village elder simply replied, "Maybe, maybe not. We will see."

Later that week, the farmer's son was trying to break the mare so it could be used in the fields. Suddenly the horse bucked, throwing the son to the ground and breaking his leg. Again, the farmer complained to the village elder, "This is terrible luck! I cannot tend to the fields myself, and this is my only son. I am ruined!"

The wise elder again seemed unmoved, and stated, "Maybe, maybe not. We will see."

This time the farmer had had enough. He lost his temper and yelled at the elder, "What do you mean maybe? My son's leg is broken. My farm will be lost! This is the worst thing that could have happened to us and you act as if it is nothing at all!"

The elder remained calm and unmoved. "Don't give up hope my friend; none of us can see the future. Everything happens as it should."

Three weeks later, the army from the farmer's province marched through the town, forcing every able-bodied young man to join the army and to march into battle. The farmer's son was not taken because of his broken leg.

The other people in the village were excited that their sons would return heroes, and exclaimed to the farmer, "It is bad luck that your son could not go to war and return a hero as well."

The farmer started to feel disgraced, but then recalled the lesson that the village elder had been trying to teach him, and replied, "Maybe, maybe not. We will see."

Two weeks later, word came to the village that the entire army was defeated in an epic battle. Not one of the young men from the village had survived. The farmer's son was the only boy of age from the village that survived this tragedy.

If you look within yourself and are sure that you have
done right, what do you have to fear or worry about?
You are required only to perform your own mission in life.
Bruce Lee

Never be in frontal opposition to any problem,
but control it by swinging with it.
Yip Man

Be master of the mind
rather than mastered by the mind.
Zen Maxim

Those who are skilled in combat do not become angered;
those who are skilled at winning do not become afraid.
Thus, the wise win before the fight,
while the ignorant fight to win.
Morihei Ueshiba

While we are resting,
the bad guys are training.
Ryron Gracie

The first priority to the ninja
is to win without fighting.
Masaaki Hatsumi

The wise hawk conceals his talons.
Japanese Proverb

A man's word is his honor.
Okinawan Proverb

No matter how many good words you read and speak of,
what good will they do you if you do not put
them into practice and use them?
Buddha

Adapt what is useful, reject what is useless,
and add what is specifically your own."
Bruce Lee

If you want to be a lion,
you must train with lions.
Carlson Gracie

The most important are the eyes.
In a real fight, if you look down out of fear,
you will certainly be defeated.
Masutatsu Oyama

In order to progress in life, one has to
improve every day in an endless process.
The Hagakure

A warrior who overreacts will rarely
finish anything successfully.
Choe Hong Hi

The essence of fighting is the
art of moving at the right time.
Bruce Lee

It is no honor for an eagle to vanquish a dove.
Italian Proverb

Noblemen discipline themselves to
be dignified at all times. Sharpen
your mind and show your dignity.
Matsura Seizen

To subdue an enemy without
fighting is the greatest of skills.
Sun Tzu

A man who has attained mastery of
an art reveals it in his every action.
Samurai Maxim

Dignity is not circumstantial.
Kotoda Yahei Toshisada

Trained fighters, much more than average people,
have an obligation to employ their skills judiciously.
To govern themselves and their emotions at all times.
Peter Hobert

You must be deadly serious in training.
Gichin Funakoshi

Focus on your one purpose.
Japanese Maxim

Opportunity is rare and a wise
man will never let it go by him.
Bayard Taylor

Training half-hearted won't build
a karate person of good character.
Kanei Uechi

It may be difficult at first,
but everything is difficult at first.
Miyamoto Musashi

Never be easily drawn into a fight.
Gichin Funakoshi

Though we are powerful and strong,
and we know how to fight,
we do not wish to fight.
Cherokee Saying

This is certain, that a man that
studies revenge keeps his wounds green,
which otherwise would heal and do well.
Francis Bacon

Never interrupt your enemy
when he is making a mistake.
Napoleon Bonaparte

He who is an ass and takes himself to be a stag,
finds his mistake when he tries to leap a ditch.
Italian Proverb

To be prepared for war is one of the
most effective means of preserving peace.
George Washington

Make yourself a sheep,
and the wolf is ready.
Russian Proverb

Your enemy is not a god.
When you are scared, so is he.
Masutatsu Oyama

Fear makes the wolf bigger than he is.
German Proverb

Mastering Awareness

One day the great sword master, Bokuden, received a visit from another sword master for whom he had great respect. He wanted to introduce his sons to the great sword master, and he also wanted to demonstrate the mastery that his sons had obtained. So he devised a small test for the young men by propping a vase on a sliding door so that it would fall on the head of anyone entering the room.

Both of the sword masters sat calmly, facing the door, and Bokuden called for his oldest son. When his son arrived, he astutely paused in front of the door, pushed it half open, and took down the vase before entering the room. He then closed the door behind him, replaced the vase, and bowed to the two masters. "This is my eldest son," said Bokuden, "he has obtained a high level and is on his way to becoming a master himself."

Then he called the next son. He slid the door open, started to enter the room, and just as the vase started to fall, he caught it. "This is my second son. He still has a long way to go, but he is making progress," declared Bokuden.

Next, he called his youngest son. He rushed into the room and the vase fell, hitting him on the back of the neck. But before the vase could hit the floor, he whirled around, drew his sword, and cut the vase in half. "This is my youngest son," said Bokuden shaking his head, "his training is lacking, but he is still young and has time to learn."

"The greatest victory is that which requires no battle." *Sun Tzu*

You could know a million techniques, but if you haven't got the mindset to use them, and you need to defend your life, or your family's life, then it's useless knowledge.
Emil Martirossian

It is foolish to try and live on past experiences. It is a very dangerous, if not fatal habit, to judge ourselves to be safe because of something that we did twenty years ago.
Charles Spurgeon

The just man is not one who does harm to none, but one whom having the power to harm represses the will.
Pythagoras

He does not guard himself well who is not always on his guard.
French Proverb

The master warrior is a man of character, a man of wisdom and insight.
Forrest E. Morgan

Doing it halfway is no good; you have to do it all the way, give yourself wholly to it.
Taisen Deshimaru

When you step beyond your own gate, you face a million enemies.
Gichin Funakoshi

The angry man will defeat
himself in battle as in life.
Samurai Maxim

Success is going from failure to failure
without loss of enthusiasm.
Winston Churchill

Wars are won by winning battles.
Battles are lost by worrying about winning the war.
Vlad Tepes

Never do an enemy a small injury.
Machiavelli

Don't think, feel. The less effort,
the faster and more powerful you will become.
Bruce Lee

Make benevolence your lifelong duty.
Gichin Funakoshi

Do not seek to follow in the footsteps
of wise men, seek what they sought.
Basho

Anger breeds confusion.
To be clear-minded you must avoid being angry.
The Bhagavad Gita

If you are not sure, don't act.
Bodhidharma

The hunter can make many mistakes,
the hunted, only one.
Native American Maxim

The body and soul of a tactician must always
be prepared for battle. If one is unprepared,
one is certainly on the way to defeat.
Kazumi Tabata

Your reality check must be done long before
you actually find yourself confronted with a
life and death, kill-or-be-killed situation.
Dirk Skinner

A fool gives full vent to his anger,
but a wise man keeps himself under control.
The Book of Proverbs

Gratitude is the sign of noble souls.
Aesop

To respond immediately to an angry
person is like throwing fuel on a fire.
Spanish Proverb

Though your enemy seems like a mouse,
watch him like a lion.
Italian Proverb

Trust in today's friends as if
they might be tomorrow's enemies.
Baltasar Gracian

A black belt is nothing more than a belt, a piece of cloth.
Your ultimate goal should not be to get your black belt.
Your ultimate goal should be to be a black belt.
Being a black belt is state of mind, a way of life.
Bohdi Sanders

The study of "principle" means training that is aimed
at reaching the highest state – mushin – in which the
mind is set free and is not caught by anything at all.
Takuan Soho

By associating with good and evil people
a man acquires the virtues and vices which
they possess, even as wind blowing over
different places takes along good and bad odors.
The Panchatantra

It is not only what we do,
but what we do not do,
for which we are accountable.
Moliere

To see what is right and
not to do it is cowardice.
Confucius

The silent person is often worth listening to.
Japanese Proverb

How often do we supply our enemies
with the means of our own destruction.
Aesop

Carelessness is a great enemy.
Japanese Proverb

If you don't overcome your tendency to
give up easily, your life will lead to nothing.
Masutatsu Oyama

To spare the ravening leopard
is an act of injustice to the sheep.
Persian Proverb

The best armor is to keep out of range.
Italian Proverb

Tomorrow's battle is won
during today's practice.
Samurai Maxim

The wise man hides his weapons.
Lao Tzu

Instead of worrying,
a strong man wears a smile.
Japanese Proverb

No matter what the warrior is doing,
he must conduct himself in the
manner of a true warrior.
Bushido Shoshinshu

Even when your spirit is calm,
do not let your body relax;
and when your body is relaxed,
do not let your spirit slacken.
Miyamoto Musashi

Virtue is more clearly shown
in the performance of fine actions
than in the nonperformance of base ones.
Aristotle

To know and to act are one and the same.
Samurai Maxim

Rely not on the likelihood of the enemy's not coming,
but on our own readiness to receive him;
not on the chance of his not attacking,
but rather on the fact that we have
made our position unassailable.
Sun Tzu

To stand still is to regress.
Gichin Funakoshi

A successful samurai should put his heart in order
first thing in the morning and last thing at night.
The Hagakure

When you see a correct course, act.
Sun Tzu

There is a best way to perform any task.
Bruce Lee

The warrior is always in training, and to some extent, at
some level of consciousness, training is always on his mind.
Forrest E. Morgan

Outside noisy, inside empty.
Chinese Proverb

Both speech and silence transgress.
Zen Maxim

Every moment of life is the last.
Basho

He who conquers others is strong;
he who conquers himself is mighty.
Lao Tzu

Great winds are powerless to
disturb the water of a deep well.
Chinese Proverb

Each action (of the warrior) is performed
from a place of fundamental wisdom...
it is completely different from the
ordinary behavior of a fool.
Even if it looks the same,
it is different on the inside.
Takuan Soho

Do nothing evil, neither in the
presence of others, nor privately.
Pythagoras

If it is not right, do not do it;
if it is not true, do not say it.
Marcus Aurelius

The man of principle never forgets
what he is, because of what others are.
Baltasar Gracian

If you want to disguise or conceal one of your intentions,
always take pains to show you have its opposite in mind,
using the strongest and most convincing reasons you can.
Francesco Guicciardini

The Tale of Two Pebbles

Long ago, in a small Indian village, a poor farmer had the misfortune of owing a large sum of money to a village moneylender. The moneylender, who was old, mean, and crooked, and fancied the farmer's beautiful daughter. So he proposed a bargain.

He said he would forgo the farmer's debt if he could marry his daughter. Both the farmer and his daughter were horrified by the proposal. So the cunning money-lender suggested that they let providence decide the matter.

He told them that he would put a black pebble and a white pebble into an empty money bag. Then the girl would have to pick one pebble from the bag.

If she picked the black pebble, she would become his wife and her father's debt would be forgiven.

If she picked the white pebble she need not marry him and her father's debt would still be forgiven.

If she refused to pick a pebble, her father would be thrown into jail.

They were standing on a pebble strewn path in the farmer's field, and, as they talked, the moneylender bent over to pick up two pebbles. As he picked them up, the sharp-eyed girl noticed that he had picked up two black pebbles, in an attempt to cheat the girl, and put them into the bag. He then asked the girl to pick a pebble from the bag.

The girl put her hand into the moneybag and drew out a pebble. Without looking at it, she fumbled and let it fall onto the path, which was full of pebbles, and it immediately became lost among all the other pebbles.

"Oh, how clumsy of me!" she said. "But never mind, if you look into the bag for the one that is left, you will be able to tell which pebble I picked."

The moneylender knew his plan had met with utter failure, as he reached in and pulled out the other black pebble. But he didn't dare argue, as that would have made his dishonesty blatantly obvious.

The farmer smiled with joy and exclaimed, "Since the remaining pebble is black, it is obvious that my daughter picked the white one!"

The moneylender could do nothing but honor his deal, since he dared not admit his dishonesty. By being aware, watchful, and witty, the girl changed what seemed to be an impossible situation into an extremely advantageous one. She was able to avoid being cheated, won her father's freedom, and escaped a lifetime of misery by her actions.

(Even the most complex problems have a solution. It is up to you to be wise enough to calm your mind and find the solution. Don't confuse worry with constructive thinking. There is always a way out; you just have to find it.)

One who is good at being a warrior
does not appear formidable.
Lao Tzu

You must carefully consider the merits of any action,
and if you then take the good and leave the bad,
your mind will naturally become more virtuous.
Takuan Soho

Reflect on this:
efforts and enemies, if left unfinished, can
both ravage you like an unextinguished fire.
Tiruvalluvar

When you see a rattlesnake poised to strike,
you do not wait until he has struck
before you crush him.
Franklin Delano Roosevelt

Life is short and no one knows
what the next moment will bring.
Dogen

You may always be victorious if you will
never enter into any contest where the
issue does not wholly depend upon yourself.
Epictetus

Only in quiet waters things mirror
themselves undistorted. Only in a quiet
mind is adequate perception of the world.
Margolis

Karate is like boiling water –
without heat, it returns to its tepid state.
Gichin Funakoshi

Even in the sheath the knife must be sharp.
Finnish Proverb

Keep your distance from unvirtuous people.
Takuan Soho

Beware a dagger hidden in a smile.
Shi Nai'an

Lay down for yourself, at the outset, a certain stamp and
type of character for yourself, which you are to maintain
whether you are by yourself or are meeting with people.
Epictetus

Hear all sides and you will be enlightened.
Hear one side, and you will be in the dark.
Wei Zheng

It isn't quite the same thing to comment
on the bull ring and to be in the bull ring.
Spanish Proverb

You have to keep your reflexes
so that when you want it, it's there.
Bruce Lee

Why blast a sparrow with a cannon.
Chinese Proverb

Right is right, even if nobody does it.
Wrong is wrong, even if everybody is wrong about it.
G. K. Chesterton

Because a human being is so malleable,
whatever one cultivates is what one becomes.
Lao Tzu

Only one who continually reexamines
himself and corrects his faults will grow.
The Hagakure

Let him who desires peace prepare for war.
Vegetius

A small hole can sink a big ship.
Russian Proverb

The warrior acts first according to
his heart and his sense of righteousness.
Kensho Furuya

It is only the tranquil mind that can allow
for fair and clear judgments free of error.
Gichin Funakoshi

So live your life that the fear of
death can never enter your heart.
Tecumseh

One sword keeps another in the sheath.
George Herbert

Every man counts as an enemy,
but not every man as a friend.
Very few can do us good,
but nearly all, harm.
Baltasar Gracian

Invincibility depends on one's self;
the enemy's vulnerability on him.
Sun Tzu

A man must decide what to do, he must go all the way,
but he must take responsibility for what he does.
No matter what he does, he must know first why he
is doing it, and then he must proceed with his
actions without having doubts or remorse about them.
Don Juan

Be careful of your thoughts;
they are the beginning of your acts.
Lao Tzu

Beware that you do not lose the
substance by grasping at the shadow.
Aesop

To return to the root is to find the meaning,
but to pursue appearances is to miss the source.
Seng Ts'an

Trust your instinct to the end,
though you can render no reason.
Ralph Waldo Emerson

We gather the consequences of our own deeds.
Garuda Purana

There is no first attack in karate.
Gichin Funakoshi

Our own heart, and not the other
men's opinion, forms our true honor.
Samuel Coleridge

Everybody who lives dies.
But not everybody who dies has lived.
Dhaggi Ramanashi

Ask questions of your heart, and you
will receive answers from your heart.
Omaha Maxim

Do not slide back two paces
when you go one step forward.
Sai Baba

Betters have their betters.
Japanese Proverb

A prudent silence is the sacred vessel of wisdom.
Baltasar Gracian

See but do not appear to see; listen but
do not appear to listen; know but do
not let it be known that you know.
Han Fei Tzu

Listen to Your Intuition

Tajima no Kami, the Shogun's sword instructor, was strolling through his garden one afternoon, completely calm and serene, contemplating the cherry blossoms. His young servant followed several steps behind him, carrying his sword. The young servant thought to himself, "It would be easy for me to kill my master at this time, as he could not see my attack and he is engrossed in the beauty of the cherry blossoms."

At that instant, Tajima no Kami turned around and looked as if he were looking for an enemy, seeking to ambush him in his own garden. He began to search his garden, looking for the danger that he sensed. Not finding anyone, he returned to his room, unable to shake the uneasy feeling that preyed on his mind.

His servant eventually asked him what was wrong, and Tajima answered, "I am disturbed by my walk in the garden. I have practiced martial arts for a long, long time, and I have developed my chokkan (intuition) to the point that I can sense when there is danger or when someone means me harm. I felt this sensation today during my walk, but I could find no danger. Not having found any danger, I am disappointed in myself. My intuition has let me down.

His servant then admitted that he had briefly entertained malicious thoughts towards his master. He humbly asked for forgiveness. Satisfied, Tajima no Kami went back outside and continued his walk, knowing that his intuition had indeed served him well.

What is necessary is never a risk.
Cardinal de Retz

At all times, look at the thing itself –
the thing behind the appearance.
Marcus Aurelius

The first law of war is to preserve
ourselves and destroy the enemy.
Mao Tse-Tung

An enemy surprised is already half-defeated.
German Proverb

When facing impossible conditions,
sometimes it is in your best interest to retreat.
The I Ching

The way is in training.
Do nothing which is not of value.
Miyamoto Musashi

It is usually the reply that causes the fight.
Japanese Proverb

He is wise who tries everything before arms.
Terence

To expect bad people not to injure others is crazy. It is to
ask the impossible. And to let them behave like that to
other people, but expect them to exempt you is arrogance.
Marcus Aurelius

In peace do not forget war.
Japanese Proverb

The more you sweat in training,
the less you bleed in battle.
Navy Seal Maxim

Practice not your art and it will soon depart.
German Proverb

Honor is sacred.
Native American Maxim

The cherry blossom among flowers,
the warrior among men.
Japanese Proverb

If you understand, things are as they are.
If you do not understand, things are as they are.
Zen Maxim

Permit no one to discover the limits of your capacities.
Never suffer another to see through you completely.
Baltasar Gracian

Pretend inferiority and encourage his arrogance.
Sun Tzu

Our real worth earns the respect
of knowledgeable people,
luck that of the public.
La Rochefoucauld

I come to you with only empty hands. I have no weapons, but should I be forced to defend myself, my principles or my honor, should it be a matter of life and death, or right or wrong; then here are my weapons, my empty hands.
Ed Parker

You need to have ferociousness in a real fight.
Masaaki Hatsumi

Relax and calm your mind.
Forget about yourself and
follow your opponent's movement.
Yip Man

If you have to kill a snake,
kill it once and for all.
Japanese Proverb

The greatest enemies, and the ones
we must mainly combat, are within.
Cervantes

How we train is how we shall respond.
Kelly S. Worden

Someone out there is training.
Law Enforcement Maxim

Unarmed hand-to-hand fighting does not change through the ages; only the name changes, and it has only one rule: do it first, do it fast, do it dirtiest.
Robert A. Heinlein

Never forget that, at the most, the teacher can give you fifteen percent of the art. The rest you have to get for yourself through practice and hard work. I can show you the path but I cannot walk it for you.
Master Tan Soh Tin

The stupid neither forgive nor forget;
the naïve forgive and forget;
the wise forgive, but do not forget.
Thomas Szasz

Try not! Do, or do not. There is no try.
Yoda

One must transcend techniques so
that the art becomes an artless art,
growing out of the unconscious.
Daisetsu Suzuki

A warrior's heart is like a sword;
it must be cleaned daily.
Billy Shearer

One who is good at battle does not get angry.
Lao Tzu

Abandoning the ego is the secret of right living.
Taisen Deshimaru

The warrior is not led by others;
but by remaining true to his convictions.
F. J. Chu

Style doesn't matter,
what works is what's important.
Mitsusuke Harada

Man is only as strong as
his convictions and beliefs.
Kensho Furuya

Calamity springs from carelessness.
Gichin Funakoshi

I have seen the best karate.
All that really matters is what
kind of human being you are.
Masami Tsuruoka

The path of the warrior is lifelong, and
mastery is often simply staying on the path.
Richard Strozzi Heckler

One should always be willing to assist others
selflessly and unconditionally by offering
one's skills and achievements to serve them.
Lao Tzu

Hide your purpose.
Baltasar Gracian

Never imagine that you are safe after
you deal a blow to your opponent.
Yagyu Tajimanokami Munenori

Courtesy should be apparent in all our actions,
words, and in all aspects of daily life.
Masutatsu Oyama

When the enemy presents an opportunity,
speedily take advantage of it.
Sun Tzu

Every single word is of
great importance to a samurai.
The Hagakura

To be prepared is half the victory.
Cervantes

One should be careful to
improve himself continually.
Shu Ching

Don't hit at all if it can be avoided,
but never hit softly.
Theodore Roosevelt

Tomorrow belongs to those
who prepare today.
African Proverb

Your greatest weapon is
in your enemy's mind.
Buddha

Violence is easy to escalate,
hard to de-escalate.
Harland Cleveland

If you are a serious warrior,
you'll become a student of anatomy.
Forrest E. Morgan

Be your friend's true friend.
The Havamal

Snakes follow the way of serpents.
Japanese Proverb

Whoso would be a man
must be a nonconformist.
Ralph Waldo Emerson

We are what we repeatedly do.
Excellence is not an act, but a habit.
Aristotle

Don't teach undesirable people.
Masaaki Hatsumi

Deprived of all else, one remains undisgraced
if still endowed with strength of character.
Tiruvalluvar

Deal with a dangerous situation while it is safe.
Eliminate what is vicious before it becomes destructive.
Lao Tzu

Having the idea is not living the reality.
Rumi

I wasn't born knowing what I teach you.
Being fond of the past, I sought it through diligence.
Confucius

If you live in the river you
should understand the crocodile.
Indian Proverb

To generalize is to be an idiot.
William Blake

PRIORITIES

A sensei stood before his class and had some items in front of him. When the class began, he silently picked up an empty one gallon mayonnaise jar and proceeded to fill it with golf balls. He then asked the students if the jar was full. They agreed that it was.

The sensei then picked up a box of pebbles and poured them into the jar. He shook the jar lightly. The pebbles rolled into the open areas between the golf balls. Once again, he asked the students if the jar was full. Again, they agreed it was.

Next he picked up a box of sand and poured it into the jar. Of course, the sand filled up everything else. And he asked once more if the jar was full, and once more the students responded with a unanimous YES!

The sensei then produced two glasses of water and poured the entire contents into the jar effectively filling the empty space between the sand.

"Now," said the sensei, "I want you to recognize that this jar represents your life. The golf balls are the important things ~ your family, your children, your health, your friends, your martial arts, your meditation, and your favorite passions, and if everything else was lost and only they remained, your life would still be full."

"The pebbles are the other things that matter like your job, your house and your car. The sand is everything else, the small stuff. If you put the sand into the jar first," he continued, "there is no room for the pebbles or the golf balls."

"The same goes for life. If you spend all your time and energy on the small stuff, you will never have room for the things that are important to you. Pay attention to the things that are critical to your happiness. Spend time with your children. Spend time with your parents. Visit with grandparents. Don't allow small things to interfere with your martial arts practice or your meditation time."

"There will always be time to clean the house and mow the lawn. Take care of your top priorities first - the things that really matter. Get your priorities straight; the rest will fall into place as it should."

One of the students raised her hand and inquired about what the water represented. The professor smiled and said, "I'm glad you asked. The water just shows you that no matter how full your life may seem, there's always room for a couple of beverages and a chat with a friend."

To every man there opens a high way and a low way,
and every man decides the way his soul will go.
John Oxenham

Don't easily trust anyone on this
earth because there are all kinds.
Bruce Lee

It is better to be a tiger for one day
than a sheep for a thousand years.
Tibetan Maxim

Never exchange a good conscience for the
good will of others, or to avoid their ill-will.
Charles Simmons

When you shoot an arrow of truth,
dip its point in honey.
Arabian Proverb

Hold yourself responsible for a higher
standard than anyone else expects of you.
Never excuse yourself.
Henry Ward Beecher

It is easier to prevent bad habits
than to break them.
Benjamin Franklin

As circumstances change,
the ways of dealing with them alter too.
Han Fei Tzu

Protecting yourself is self-defense.
Protecting others is warriorship.
Bohdi Sanders

A warrior is worthless unless he rises above others
and stands strong in the midst of the storm.
The Hagakure

Do not exhibit your sore finger for all to strike upon,
and do not complain of it, for malice always
pounds where it hurts most.
Baltasar Gracian

What is not increased diminishes.
Rumi

When you arise in the morning, give thanks for the
morning light, for your life and strength. Give thanks
for your food and the joy of living. If you see no
reason for giving thanks, the fault lies in yourself.
Tecumseh

Ikken hisatsu, one punch kill, is the essence of karate.
Put everything, your whole life, into one punch.
Masami Tsuruoka

Who with the wolf associates, to howl learns.
Bulgarian Proverb

Thatch your roof before rainy weather;
dig your well before you are thirsty.
Chinese Proverb

When the world is at peace,
a gentleman keeps his sword by his side.
Wu Tsu

The only thing necessary for the triumph of evil
is for good men to do nothing
Edmund Burke

Defeat is a state of mind;
no one is ever defeated until
defeat has been accepted as a reality.
Bruce Lee

If your temper rises, withdraw your hand;
if your hand rises, withdraw your temper.
Gojun Miyagi

Never separate yourself from
the way of the warrior.
Miyamoto Musashi

The traditional forms must be practiced correctly;
real combat is another matter.
Gichin Funakoshi

Treat every encounter as a fight to the finish.
The Eight Essentials for Novice Swordsmen

One should have learning on the left
and the martial arts on the right.
Hojo Nagauji

Do not show any intention.
Gichin Funakoshi

A just man.
He stands on the side of right with such conviction,
that neither the passion of the mob, nor the violence of
a despot can make him overstep the bounds of reason.
Baltasar Gracian

Warriors aren't born, and they aren't made...
they create themselves through trial and error and
by their ability to conquer their own frailties and faults.
Philip J. Messina

Do not think dishonestly.
Miyamoto Musashi

It is truly regrettable that a person will
treat a man who is valuable to him well,
and a man who is worthless to him poorly.
Hojo Shigetoki

Every action we take, everything we do,
is either a victory or defeat in the struggle
to become what we want to be.
Anne Byrhhe

We ought to do everything both
cautiously and confidently at the same time.
Epictetus

One bad example destroys
more than twenty good.
Hungarian Proverb

Never do anything against conscience
even if the state demands it.
Albert Einstein

The word friend is common, the fact is rare.
Phaedrus

The Fence

There once was a young boy who had a bad temper. His father gave him a bag of nails and told him that every time he lost his temper, he must hammer a nail into the fence.

The first day the boy had driven 37 nails into the fence. Over the next few weeks as he learned to control his anger, the number of nails hammered daily, gradually dwindled down. He discovered it was easier to hold his temper than to drive those nails into the fence.

Finally the day came when the boy didn't lose his temper at all. Excited at his victory, he told his father about it and the father suggested that the boy now pull out one nail for each day that he was able to hold his temper. The days passed and the young boy was finally able to tell his father that all the nails were gone.

The father took his son by the hand and led him to the fence. He said "You have done well, my son, but look at the holes in the fence. The fence will never be the same as it once was. When you say or do things in anger, you leave a scar, much like the holes you have left in this fence."

(You can put a knife in a man and draw it out. It won't matter how many times you say I'm sorry, the wound or scar is still there. Make sure you control your temper the next time you are tempted to say or do something you will later regret.)

Highly evolved people have
their own conscience as pure law.
Lao Tzu

It is not the oath that makes us believe
the man, but the man the oath.
Aeschylus

The superior man is watchful
over himself even when alone.
Chung Yung

The superior man does not give up good conduct
because the inferior man rails against him.
Hsun-Tzu

It is no easy thing for a principle to
become a man's own unless each day
he maintains it and works it out in his life.
Epictetus

Knowing is not enough, we must apply.
Willing is not enough, we must do.
Goethe

Do nothing to make you
lose respect for yourself.
Baltasar Gracian

The superior man is governed by decorum;
the inferior man is ruled by law.
Confucius

Though the wind blows,
the mountain does not move.
Japanese Proverb

Warriors should never be
thoughtless or absentminded
but handle all things with forethought.
Shiba Yoshimasa

Perceive things that are not obvious.
Miyamoto Musashi

What I must do is all that concerns me,
not what the people think.
Ralph Waldo Emerson

For when moral value is considered,
the concern is not the actions, which are seen,
but rather with their inner principles,
which are not seen.
Kant

The wise man never trusts in appearances.
Confucius

We are all ready to be savage in some cause.
The difference between a good man and
a bad one is the choice of the cause.
William James

Wise men do not argue with idiots.
Japanese Proverb

He who plants a forest in the morning
cannot expect to saw planks the same evening.
Chinese Proverb

No weapon is sharper than the mind;
even the finest sword is inferior.
The Masters of Huainan

One should practice steadfast
and indiscriminative virtue without
demanding others to do the same in return.
Lao Tzu

The wise pursue understanding;
fools follow the reports of others.
Tibetan Proverb

It is the task of a good man
to help those in misfortune.
Sophocles

He is the best man who, when making his plans,
fears and reflects on everything that can happen to him,
but in the moment of action is bold.
Herodotus

To avoid action when justice is at
stake demonstrates a lack of courage.
Gichin Funakoshi

Patience is also a form of action.
Auguste Rodin

He has honor if he holds himself to an ideal
of conduct though it is inconvenient,
unprofitable, or dangerous to do so.
Walter Lippmann

What lies in our power to do,
it lies in our power not to do.
Aristotle

If you calm your own mind and discern
the inner minds of others, that may
be called the foremost art of war.
Shiba Yoshimasa

The wise man adapts
himself to the circumstances.
Confucius

More satisfying by far,
that many depend upon you,
than that you depend upon anybody.
Baltasar Gracian

Truth is not a matter of personal viewpoint.
Vernon Howard

In strategy, secrecy is esteemed.
Japanese Proverb

Put your heart, mind, intellect, and
soul even to your smallest acts.
Swami Sivananda

A journey of a thousand miles
begins with one step.
Lao Tzu

Convince the world by your character.
Chief John Ross

What is of supreme importance in war
is to attack the enemy's strategy.
Sun Tzu

The secret of success is before attempting anything,
be very clear about why you are doing it.
Guan Yin Tzu

Chance is a word void of sense;
nothing can exist without a cause.
Voltaire

Able to be calm, then able to respond.
Xunzi

Listening to only one side creates prejudice.
Japanese Maxim

Distinguish the man of words
from the man of deeds.
Baltasar Gracian

Attack where he is unprepared;
move when he does not expect you.
Sun Tzu

The Secret of Heaven and Hell

A samurai named Nobushige, came to the Zen master Hakuin, and asked him for the secret of Heaven and Hell.

"Who are you?" asked Hakuin.

"I am a samurai," Nobushige answered proudly, "I follow the way of the warrior and I wish to know the secrets of the afterlife."

"You, a samurai," Hakuin said with a sarcastic tone. "What fool would hire the likes of you? You look more like a beggar than a samurai!"

Nobushige became so angry that he began to draw his sword, as no samurai would permit such an insult. But Hakuin continued, "You seem to be nothing more than a man who plays with a sword. Your sword is probably too dull to cut cooked rice!"

At this Nobushige was ready to cut the Zen master down, but as he drew his sword, Hakuin quickly said, "Here opens the gates of Hell."

At these words, the proud samurai perceived the master's lesson, returned his sword to his scabbard, and bowed to Hakuin.

As the samurai bowed, Hakuin said with a peaceful smile, "Here opens the gates of Heaven."

Always think in terms of
what the other person wants.
James Van Fleet

No battle's won in bed.
The Havamal

Be slow of tongue and quick of eye.
Cervantes

You always win by not saying
the things you don't need to say.
Chinese Proverb

Lower your voice and
strengthen your argument.
Lebanon Proverb

Do not let trifles disturb your tranquility of mind.
Ignore the inconsequential.
Grenville Kleiser

Deliberate often – Decide once.
Latin Proverb

Seek the counsel of the aged, for their eyes
have looked on the faces of the years and
their ears have hearkened to the voices of life.
Kahlil Gibran

It is essential to cultivate the warrior spirit.
Saito Totsudo

Don't follow any advice, no matter how good,
until you feel as deeply in your spirit as you
think in your mind, that the counsel is wise.
David Seabury

Justice is the virtue of warriorhood,
the root of martial arts.
Nakae Toju

Think like a man of action,
act like a man of thought.
Thomas Mann

Do not forget great kindness,
even for a single meal.
Emperor Wen Di

If you are always getting angry, you
will turn your nature against the Way.
Bodhidharma

Take a deep breath of life and
consider how it should be lived.
Don Quixote's Creed

In the midst of men who hate us,
let us live without hatred.
The Dhammapada

A hero in old age never
lets go of his principles.
Cao Cao

Faces we see, hearts we know not.
Spanish Proverb

My enemy is not the man who wrongs me,
but the man who means to wrong me.
Democritus

Sow confusion to reap certainty.
Spartacus

The wise live among people,
but are indifferent to their praise or blame.
Chuang Tzu

Muddy water, let stand, becomes clear.
Lao Tzu

Those who do good because they want
to be seen to be good are not good.
Lieh Tzu

Honor is central to warriorship.
Forrest E. Morgan

Never be easily drawn into a fight.
Gichin Funakoshi

Desire no revenge.
Masaaki Hatsumi

Discipline, not desire,
determines your destiny.
Bud Malmstrom

The end and perfection of our victories is to avoid the
vices and infirmities of those whom we subdue.
Alexander the Great

A rule of thumb for a warrior is that he makes his
decisions so carefully that nothing that may happen as a
result of them can surprise him, much less drain his power.
Carlos Castaneda

In dangerous times wise men say nothing.
Aesop

No man ever becomes wise by chance.
Seneca

Remember how lucky you are to live in a time of
peace and plenty, but prepare for worse times.
Code of the Samurai

Control your mind and remain undisturbed.
That is the secret of perfect peace.
Sai Baba

Never walk away from home ahead of
your axe and sword. You can't feel a
battle in your bones or foresee a fight.
The Havamal

Reputation often spills less blood.
Samurai Maxim

The way of a warrior is based on humanity, love,
and sincerity; the heart of martial valor is true
bravery, wisdom, love, and friendship.
Morihei Ueshiba

Things are not always what they seem;
the first appearance deceives many;
the intelligence of a few perceives
what has been carefully hidden.
Phaedrus

Don't follow the advice of others; rather,
learn to listen to the voice within yourself.
Dogen

When you have to kill a man,
it costs nothing to be polite.
Winston Churchill

Rage and resentment lead to rash action.
Sun Tzu

Rediscover natural compassion.
Lao Tzu

Focus on making yourself better,
not on thinking that you are better.
Bohdi Sanders

Certain good qualities are like the senses:
people entirely lacking in them can
neither perceive nor comprehend them.
La Rochefoucauld

No day unalert; fate likes to play the buffoon, and to upset
everything unawares in order to catch the sleeping;
always stand ready for inspection in spirit,
in mind, in fortitude, even in appearance.
Baltasar Gracian

You must not show your weak points,
either in the martial arts or in everyday life.
Taisen Deshimaru

There is no such thing as a fair fight.
Bohdi Sanders

The more quickly brought to anger,
the more quickly brought to death.
Chinese Maxim

The world is a dangerous place,
not because of those who do evil, but
because of those who look on and do nothing.
Albert Einstein

Don't protect people who don't deserve it.
Your job is to protect the good.
Observe one's true character.
Masaaki Hatsumi

To be prepared beforehand for any
contingency is the greatest of virtues.
Sun Tzu

In war there is no substitute for victory.
Douglas MacArthur

True Budo has an overwhelming emphasis
on the development of moral character.
Glenn Morris

In critical times,
one must be utterly
devoted to the cause of justice.
Gichin Funakoshi

Adversity is a mirror that
reveals one's true self.
Chinese Proverb

All men make mistakes,
but a good man yields when he knows
his course is wrong, and repairs the evil.
Sophocles

A wise man, in great or small matters,
must act with due consideration.
Sakya Pandit

Brave hearts do not back down.
Euripides

The brave and generous have the best lives.
They're seldom sorry.
The Havamal

He who lives without discipline,
dies without honor.
Icelandic Proverb

Even if the stream is shallow,
wade it as if it were deep.
Korean Proverb

If you are forced into a position in which you
must either hurt or be hurt, be sure to make
your move before someone else does.
Francesco Guicciardini

Bushido:
The Way of the Warrior

I see things through different eyes.
I see a bigger picture when others see grey skies.
Though many can't conceive it, I stand, facing the wind.
My bravery is not from my skills, but from my inner strength.
I am a warrior; I'll walk the extra mile.
Not because I have to, but because it's worth my while.
I know that I am different when I stand on a crowded street.
I know the fullness of winning; I've tasted the cup of defeat.
I am a warrior; they say I walk with ease.
Though trained for bodily harm, my intentions are for peace.
The world may come and go, but a different path I'll choose.
A path I will not stray from, no matter win or lose.

(Anonymous)

The Martial Way

The Martial Way does not start and end at the door of the training hall. It is a way of life in which every action, in and out of the training hall, is done in the context of warriorship.

The Martial Way is a way of living. It is a holistic discipline aimed at the pursuit of excellence, not just in the training hall, but at life. Its disciples strive to apply the Way in every vocation, and its adepts tend to be achievers in any field of endeavor. One lives The Martial Way.

Forrest E. Morgan

You can also commit injustice by doing nothing.
Marcus Aurelius

Moderation in temper is always a virtue;
but moderation in principle is always a vice.
Thomas Paine

Let the wise man take refuge in his silence.
Baltasar Gracian

Individuals create karma;
karma does not create individuals.
Bodhidharma

Shun any action that will diminish honor.
Tiruvalluvar

A warrior faces a double challenge: confronting the evil of
others while resisting the darkness within. If he gives in
to the latter, he becomes nothing more than a thug.
Wim Demeere

The Universal Way is not just
a matter of speaking wisdom,
but one of continual practice.
Lao Tzu

Never enrich a man to the point where
He can afford to turn against you;
never ennoble a man to the point
where he becomes a threat.
Han Fei Tzu

The success of very important matters
often depends on doing or not doing
something that seems trivial.
Francesco Guicciardini

In whatever position you find yourself,
determine first your objective.
Marshall Ferdinand Foch

Better be proficient in one art
than a smatterer in a thousand.
Japanese Proverb

Would you persuade,
speak of interest, not of reason.
Benjamin Franklin

What you wish others to do, do yourself.
Ramakrishna

There is much to be considered
before the sword is drawn.
Baltasar Gracian

It is necessary to the happiness of man
that he be mentally faithful to himself.
Thomas Paine

When the time comes that foes pose as friends,
keep a friendly face but banish their
brotherhood from your heart.
Tiruvalluvar

Neither anger nor fear shall
find lodging in your mind.
Dekanawidah

We must not be innocents abroad
in a world that is not innocent.
George Washington

We should live as though our life
would be both long and short.
Bias

For one word a man is often deemed to be wise,
and for one word he is often deemed to be foolish.
Confucius

There are more bad men than good.
Francesco Guicciardini

The pebble in the brook secretly
thinks itself a precious stone.
Japanese Proverb

If you do not guard the door,
if you do not make fast the gate,
then tigers will lurk there.
Han Fei Tzu

What we do upon some great occasion will probably
depend on what we already are; and what we already are
will be the result of previous years of self-discipline.
Percy Bysshe Shelley

Do not let what you cannot do
interfere with what you can do.
John Wooden

If you are not training seriously,
you are just wasting time.
Minoru Inaba

All warfare is based on deception.
Sun Tzu

Method is more important than strength,
when you wish to control your enemies.
Nagarjuna

Kill the spider and you
will destroy the cobweb.
Maltese Proverb

Trust in God, but tie your camel.
Arabian Proverb

Listen to your intuition and realize
when the first attack has taken place.
Bohdi Sanders

Quiet your body. Quiet your mind.
Buddha

Depend on others and you will go hungry.
Nepalese Proverb

Silence is the cornerstone of character.
Ohiyesa

Cattle die, and kinsmen die,
And so one dies one's self;
But a noble name will never die,
If good renown one gets.
The Havamal

Feel your confidence and see yourself winning.
Always see yourself winning.
Loren W. Christensen

Perception is strong and sight is weak.
Miyamoto Musashi

There is nothing on this earth more
to be prized than true friendship.
Saint Thomas of Aquinas

Never admit defeat, even if you have been wounded.
The good soldier's wounds spur him to gather his strength.
Desiderius Erasmus

A promise is a debt.
Irish Proverb

Nothing is better or surer than fixing
things in such a way that you are safe,
not because your enemy is unwilling,
but because he is unable to hurt you.
Francesco Guicciardini

Pardon the other man's faults
but deal strictly with your own.
Sai Baba

However troubled the times,
men of imperturbable perception
never commit shameful or sordid deeds.
Tiruvalluvar

To compose our character is our duty.
Montaigne

Great spirits have always encountered
violent opposition from mediocre minds.
Albert Einstein

One kind word warms three winter months.
Japanese Proverb

He who wants to sell his honor
will always find a buyer.
Arabian Proverb

You can't please everybody.
Aesop

The warrior backs up his words
with conviction and action.
Tony L. Jones

The true victory is defeat of your base nature.
Gojun Miyagi

To be a samurai is to be polite at all times.
Hojo Nagauji

Understand the spirit of those with whom you deal...the
man of passion always speaks of matters far differently
from what they are... thus does everyone babble according
to his feelings or his moods, and all, very far from the truth.
Baltasar Gracian

Spirit of the Sword

A Bushido maxim proclaims that the sword is the soul of the samurai. It is a symbol of virility, loyalty, and courage, and the preferred weapon of the samurai warriors. According to the samurai, the sword can be benevolent or malevolent, depending on the spirit of both the sword maker and the sword owner.

This philosophy states that the sword is an extension of the person who owns it and vibrates in sync with the energy of the owner. Because of this, the inner spirit and harmony of both the sword smith and the owner are considered very important. Before forging a sword, the master sword maker would spend several days in meditation, cleanse himself with cold water, dress in white, and then set to work creating the sword with both his energy and skill.

In the beginning of the sixteenth century, Masamune and Murasama were both considered to be two of the best sword makers, making swords of great quality. Murasama was known to be a violent man of intimidating stature. He had a reputation for forging swords that always seemed to be used in bloody combat.

On the other hand, Masamune was known to be a man of calm serenity, who performed cleansing rituals before forging his blades. He took great effort to ensure that his swords were made with the correct spirit and contained the right energy.

One day a great Shogun asked both sword makers if they would be willing to test the quality of their swords in order to demonstrate the difference in the quality of each of their methods. They both agreed.

In order to test the quality of the swords, the Shogun had his servant place Murasama's sword in the nearby stream. As leaves floated down the stream, they were instantly cut in half as they came into contact with Murasama's sword.

The Shogun then had Masamune's sword put into the stream. The leaves floated down the stream towards the blade, but always seemed to avoid the blade and float to one side or the other. Not a single leaf was cut by Masamune's sword. Each one floated past the blade as if the sword itself wanted to cause them no harm.

Then the Shogun gave his thoughts on the two swords. The Murasama sword is terrible because it has a violent and destructive energy. The Masamune sword is enlightened and is able to triumph without cutting.

A hundred lifetimes may not be enough to rectify
the mistake made in one short morning.
Chinese Proverb

The superior man must always
remain himself in all situations of life.
Chung Yung

Those skilled at making the enemy move do so by
creating a situation to which he must conform.
Sun Tzu

The character of every act depends on
the circumstances in which it is done.
Oliver Wendell Holmes

Victorious warriors win first and then go to war,
defeated warriors go to war first then seek to win.
Sun Tzu

Perfection is attained by slow degrees;
she requires the hand of time.
Voltaire

Let what works well be the test for what is right.
Bruce Lee

Virtue, then, is a state of character concerned with choice.
Aristotle

A man's action is only a picture book of his creed.
Ralph Waldo Emerson

The steadfastness of the wise is but the art of
keeping their agitation locked in their hearts.
La Rochefoucauld

When nothing can be done about the way things are,
the wise stop worrying about the situation.
Lao Tzu

Courage is resistance to fear,
mastery of fear – not absence of fear.
Mark Twain

A man has no more character than
he can command in a time of crisis.
Ralph W. Sockman

When walking, walk. When eating, eat.
Zen Maxim

Just as a stick must be either straight or crooked,
so a man must be either just or unjust.
Zeno the Stoic

Surprise defeats strength and speed.
Glenn Morris

The very first step in self-restraint
is the restraint of thoughts.
Gandhi

Don't tell your secret even to a fence.
Irish Proverb

Do every act of your life as if it were your last.
Marcus Aurelius

Even Time, the father of all,
cannot undo what has been
done, whether right or wrong.
Pindar

Most of the time, we are only partially alive.
Marcel Proust

Until you have rectified yourself,
you cannot rectify others.
Chinese Proverb

As a human being one should train
one's mind and one's ability to the fullest.
Miyamoto Musashi

Never trust your tongue
when your heart is bitter.
Samuel J. Hurwitt

The wise conquer by strength,
rather than anger.
Nagarjuna

Victory is not gained through idleness
German Proverb

An angry warrior is never a conscious warrior.
Scott Shaw

Train with the energy of a warrior and
soon you will have the heart of a warrior.
Yan Lei

When you react, you let others control you.
When you respond, you are in control.
Bohdi Sanders

One who is a samurai should
continually read the ancient records
so that he may strengthen his character.
Code of the Samurai

Feel the warrior within you.
Loren W. Christensen

Living well is the best revenge.
George Herbert

One has to face fear or forever run from it.
Hawk

Warriorhood is action, not good intentions.
Martina Sprague

The future is purchased by the present.
French Proverb

Never underestimate an adversary.
Kazumi Tabata

Man lives freely only by his readiness to die.
Gandhi

I do what is mine to do;
the rest does not disturb me.
Marcus Aurelius

The surest possession is real contentment.
Nagarjuna

One should constantly be
in a state of preparedness.
Hironori Otsuka

Good means not merely not to do wrong,
but rather not to desire to do wrong.
Democritus

In inner quiet lies the salvation of the spirit.
Baltasar Gracian

You must be the change
you wish to see in the world.
Ganhdi

Obsessed is a word the lazy use
to describe the dedicated.
Mike Reeves

A young man owes respect and
gratitude to his father and elders.
Leon Battista Alberti

To do two things at once is to do neither.
Syrus

A righteous man is cautious in friendship.
The Book of Proverbs

Self-knowledge is the
beginning of self-improvement.
Spanish Proverb

The Farmer and the Snake

There is an old Japanese folk tale about the farmer and the snake which would serve you well to remember. The farmer was out working on his farm one day, getting ready for the winter snows to set in. It was already cold and snow was on the ground. While doing his chores, he came across a snake lying in the snow, nearly frozen to death. Feeling benevolent, the farmer wrapped the snake in his coat and took it inside his home to see if he could save the poor creature.

The farmer laid the snake on the floor in front of the fireplace to warm it up and see if he could revive it. He checked on it often to see if it was going to live or not. As the snake started to show a bit of life, the farmer went into the kitchen to get some water for his new friend. Coming back into the room with the saucer of water, the farmer leaned over and placed the water in front of the snake. In a split second, the snake lunged out and bit the farmer in the neck, rendering a lethal dose of toxic venom.

As he lay on the floor, dying from the venomous bite, the farmer looked at the snake and asked, "Why did you kill me after I saved your life?" The snake coldly said, as it slithered away, "I can't help it, it's just my nature."

(Learn to judge the nature of others. There are many bad people out there who will take advantage of any help you offer, and then stab you in the back. Help others when you can, but be selective about who you help and what you get yourself into. See things as they truly are, not as you want them to be.)

Given enough time, any man may master the physical.
With enough knowledge, any man may become wise.
It is the true warrior who can master both.
Tien T'ai

Thou shalt not be a victim.
Thou shalt not be a perpetrator.
Above all, thou shalt not be a bystander.
Holocaust Museum

Anger at a petty offense is unworthy of a superior man,
but indignation for a great cause is righteous wrath.
Mencius

It is better to sleep on things beforehand
than lie awake about them afterwards.
Baltasar Gracian

Those who know the least obey the best.
Farquhar

Habits change into character.
Ovid

If a battle cannot be won, do not fight it.
Sun Tzu

Intimidation is a state of mind.
Loren W. Christensen

A wise man stumbles once over a peg.
Pashto

A wise man fights to win, but he is twice a fool
who has no plan for possible defeat.
Louis L'amour

Self-discipline is the
cornerstone of any endeavor.
Bohdi Sanders

From him to whom much is given,
much shall be expected.
Jesus

Few men are brave by nature,
but good order and experience make many so.
Niccolo Machiavelli

A man cannot be too careful
in the choice of his enemies.
Oscar Wilde

When the enemy presents an opportunity,
speedily take advantage of it.
Sun Tzu

The sure way to excel in anything, is only to have a close
and undissipated attention while you are about it.
Lord Chesterfield

Sword and mind must be united.
Technique by itself is insufficient,
and spirit alone is not enough.
Yamada Jirokichi

You can better rely on someone
who needs you or who happens to
have a common objective, than
on someone you have benefited.
For men are generally not grateful.
Francesco Guicciardini

He who has mastered the "art" does not have to use
his sword; he compels his adversary to kill himself.
Tajima No Kami

Know the chink in your armor.
Baltasar Gracian

Do not let your power be seen;
be blank and actionless.
Han Fei Tzu

A hero is one who values honor, disregards
life and death, and then practices the principles.
He courageously does not submit to anything.
Kazumi Tabata

Remember to make a great difference
between companions and friends.
Lord Chesterfield

A true warrior is always armed with three things:
the radiant sword of pacification,
the mirror of bravery, wisdom and friendship,
and the precious jewel of enlightenment.
Morihei Ueshiba

Since karate exists for cultivating the spirit
and training the body, it must be a moral
way surpassing mere techniques.
Masutatsu Oyama

Countless acts that seem ridiculous
have hidden reasons that are
exceedingly wise and sound.
La Rochefoucauld

Keep your broken arm inside your sleeve.
Chinese Proverb

There is no finish line.
When you reach one goal, find a new one.
Chuck Norris

Though many people talk about war,
very few buckle on armor.
Han Fei Tzu

He who lacks foresight and underestimates
his enemy will surely be captured by him.
Sun Tzu

True victory is self-victory.
Japanese Proverb

Expect the best.
Prepare for the worst.
Capitalize on what comes.
Zig Ziglar

The final goal of judo is to perfect yourself and
contribute something of value to the world.
Jigoro Kano

As the stamp of great minds is to
suggest much in few words, so,
contrariwise, little minds have the gift
of talking a great deal and saying nothing.
La Rochefoucauld

Through training, we realize that anger is a
waste of energy, that it has only negative
effects on the self and others.
Jigoro Kano

Subjecting yourself to vigorous training is
more for the sake of forging a resolute spirit
than it is for developing a strong body.
Masutatsu Oyama

Man is a moving being.
If he does not move to what is good,
he will surely move to what is not.
The Demon's Sermon on the Martial Arts

Do not be the victim of first impressions.
Baltasar Gracian

You can neither protect nor defend yourself
against criticism; you have to act in defiance
of it and this is gradually accepted.
Johann Wolfgang von Goethe

The knowledge of mankind is a very useful knowledge for everybody. You will have to do with all sorts of characters; you should therefore know them thoroughly, in order to manage them ably.
Lord Chesterfield

When a student is honest,
he is responsible to himself first.
Jhoon Rhee

Know the enemy and know yourself; in a hundred battles you will never be in peril. When you are ignorant of the enemy but know yourself, your chances of winning or losing are equal. If ignorant both of your enemy and of yourself, you are certain in every battle to be in peril.
Sun Tzu

It is far safer to be feared than to be loved.
Niccolo Machiavelli

Let cold deliberation take the place of sudden outburst. The first step in rising to anger is to note that you are angry, for that is to enter mastery of the situation. Fine proof of judgment to keep your head when the fools have lost theirs: every flair of temper is a step downwards from the rational.
Baltasar Gracian

It is not difficult to know a thing;
what is difficult is to know is
how to use what you know.
Han Fei Tzu

The Fisherman and the Samurai

A long time ago, during the reign of the Tokagawa Shogunate, a samurai set out on an errand. Precisely one year ago to the day, he had lent ten koku to a fisherman in a small coastal village nearby, and today was the day the fisherman had promised he would repay the debt.

The samurai arrived in the village at noon and upon inquiring at the fisherman's home he was told by the fisherman's wife that he would find the man down at his boat working on his nets. Upon seeing the samurai coming up the beach the fisherman threw himself to the ground and bowed his head to the sand.

"Get up," said the samurai, "As agreed, it has been one year and I have come to collect the money you owe me."

"I have not forgotten my debt to you," said the fisherman, who now stood, but with his head still bowed, "but it has been a very bad year for me and I regret that I do not have the money I owe you."

Hearing this, the samurai, who was not a man known for his patience, flushed with anger and quickly drew his sword, preparing to kill the fisherman then and there. "Why should I not simply slay you?" shouted the samurai as he raised the deadly blade above his head.

Fearing that his life was at an end, and having nothing to lose, the fisherman boldly spoke out. "For some time now I have been studying martial arts," he replied, "and one of the lessons that my master teaches, is never to strike when you are angry. I beg you, give me one more year to pay you what I owe."

Thinking about what the fisherman had just said, the samurai slowly lowered his sword. "Your master is wise," said the samurai, "as a student of the art of the sword, I too have heard that lesson many times, but sometimes I get so angry that I act without thinking."

Putting away his sword the samurai spoke in a voice that was used to being obeyed. "You shall have another year to repay your debt to me," he said, "but when I return if you do not have all the money you owe me I shall not hesitate to take your life instead."

Having left the village later than he intended to, it was already dark by the time the samurai arrived home. Seeing no lights on in the house, he crept in quietly, not wishing to wake the servants or his wife. As he entered his bed chamber, he noticed that there were two people lying on his futon, one he recognized as his wife and the other from his clothing was unmistakably another samurai.

Swiftly he drew his sword, and as his anger quickly grew, he moved in to slay them both. Just then, as he was about to strike, the fisherman's words came back to him, "never strike when you are angry." This time I shall follow the lesson, he thought to himself. Pausing, he took a deep breath and tried to relax, and then on purpose he made a loud noise.

Hearing the sound, both his wife and the stranger immediately woke up. When his wife heard him and lit a candle, he found himself face to face with his wife and his mother, who had dressed up in his clothes and had laid another set of swords next to her. "What is the meaning of this," he demanded, "I almost slew you both."

His wife quickly explained that when he had not returned by night fall, they decided to dress his mother up in his clothes, so in the event that an intruder entered the home, he would be frightened off at the sight of a samurai in the house. At that moment the samurai realized that his habit of "striking without thinking" had almost cost him the life of his wife and his beloved mother.

One year later, the samurai again walked down the same beach towards the fisherman. After exchanging the proper formal greetings, the fisherman said, "It has been an excellent year my Lord, here is all the money I owe you, as promised, and with interest."

"Keep your money," replied the samurai, "You do not know it, but your debt was paid to me long ago."

Life is available only in the present moment.
Thich Nhat Hanh

Seven times fall, eight times get up.
Be stronger in your mind and spirit.
Fumio Demura

Never refuse or hesitate to take steps
against impending dangers because
you think they are too late.
Francesco Guicciardini

In planning, never a useless move;
in strategy, no step taken in vain.
Sun Tzu

The man who would be a warrior considers it
his most basic intention to keep death always
in mind. When one constantly keeps death in
mind, both loyalty and filial piety are realized.
In addition, even his character is improved.
Daidoji Yuzan

Never leave an enemy standing.
Shaka Zulu

Prepare yourself in good fortune for the bad.
Baltasar Gracian

The mind is a powerful factor
in everything you do.
Joe Hyams

The sage does not try to practice the ways of antiquity or
to abide by a fixed standard, but examines the affairs
of the age and takes what precautions are necessary.
Han Fei Tzu

Nurture the ability to perceive truth in all matters.
Miyamoto Musashi

The enemy must not know where I intend to give battle.
For if he does not know where I intend to give battle,
he must prepare in a great many places.
Sun Tzu

To convert petty annoyances into matters of importance,
is to become seriously involved in nothing.
Baltasar Gracian

I refuse to lower my standards to
accommodate those who refuse to raise theirs.
Steve Gamlin

No one saves us but ourselves.
No one can and no one will.
We ourselves must walk the path.
Buddha

True strength is not
always shown through victory.
Rickson Gracie

In hardship you know your friends.
Japanese Proverb

Make your enemy think that your normal force is
extraordinary, and your extraordinary is your normal.
Sun Tzu

Look beneath. For ordinary things are far other than they
seem. The false is ever the lead in everything, continually
dragging along the fools: the truth brings up the rear,
is late, and limps along upon the arm of time.
Baltasar Gracian

Warriors are not always the fastest or the strongest men.
Strength and speed can be developed through training.
Warriors are those who choose to stand between their
enemy and all that he loves or holds sacred.
(anonymous)

Always remember not to adhere to one technique.
Masaaki Hatsumi

It is foolish to get angry with people
whose power is so great that you can
never hope to avenge yourself. Even if
they offend you, therefore, grin and bear it.
Francesco Guicciardini

A footprint is left by a sandal,
but is the footprint the sandal?
Japanese Proverb

Do not engage with him who has nothing to lose.
Baltasar Gracian

When you see the correct course, act.
Sun Tzu

In extreme situations, unity of mind
and technique are essential.
Do not let your heart waver.
Morihei Ueshiba

Old and young, we are all on our last cruise.
Robert Louis Stevenson

Let others say their piece –
I will gain knowledge thereby.
Han Fei Tzu

Mental bearing – calmness – not skill,
is the sign of a matured Samurai.
Japanese Proverb

Our fears don't stop death; they stop life.
Rickson Gracie

Wisdom is not in words;
it is in understanding.
Hazrat Inayat Khan

When you perform kata, the most
important thing is your mental attitude.
Gogen Yamaguchi

To understand your fear
is the beginning of really seeing.
Bruce Lee

To let your guard down
is tantamount to suicide.
Masaaki Hatsumi

The goal of a battle is to conquer
the opponent's fighting spirit.
When the opponent loses his fighting spirit,
that's the end of the battle.
Minoru Inaba

It is you who must make the effort;
the sages can only teach.
The Dhammapada

When the eagle attacks,
he dives without extending his wings.
When the tiger is about to leap on his prey,
he crawls with his ears laid back.
By the same token, when a sage is
at the point of acting, no one can sense it.
Gichin Funakoshi

Karate is not something so simple
as to teach only fighting.
Kanei Uechi

Learning defense improves the attack.
If the lion knows how the prey can escape,
it'll capture it in a more precise way.
Rillion Gracie

The instant a warrior confronts a foe,
all things come into focus.
Morihei Ueshiba

No matter what you do,
you have to have a fine character as a man.
Meitoku Yagi

Mental bearing, calmness, not skill,
is the sign of a matured samurai.
Japanese Proverb

The best fighter is not a boxer, karate or judo man.
The best fighter is someone who can adapt on any style.
He kicks too good for a boxer, throws too good for a
karate man, and punches too good for a judo man.
Bruce Lee

Foster and polish the warrior spirit while serving in the
world; illuminate the path according to your inner light.
Morihei Ueshiba

If you push yourself, if you go on a journey of learning,
then you will finally discover yourself. Not only will you
know yourself, but you will become one with your spirit.
Emil Martirossian

When you find your inner peace through meditation,
you can carry it everywhere with every
waking moment, even into war.
Master Wu

Most of our information is gathered
by our eyes. It is important to train our
eyes to look properly and effectively.
William Cheung

Soft kata will produce fast
and disappearing movement.
Kuroda Tetsuzan

Put karate into your everyday living;
that is how you will see its true beauty.
Gichin Funakoshi

Always observe your opponent carefully
during the first seconds of every encounter.
Masaaki Hatsumi

Inner mental technique is more
important than the physical one.
Gichin Funakoshi

You must concentrate upon and consecrate
yourself wholly to each day, as though
a fire were raging in your hair.
Taisen Deshimaru

The path of martial arts
begins and ends with courtesy.
So be genuinely polite on every occasion.
Masutatsu Oyama

If you have to think about a technique,
you haven't done it enough.
Norman Harris

A negative frame of mind runs counter
to the principle of maximum efficiency.
Jigoro Kano

Refrain from reckless and thoughtless actions.
Be as calm and judicious as a mountain.
General Choi

For the choke, there are no tough guys.
Helio Gracie

One who is impatient in trivial matters,
can seldom achieve success in
matters of great importance.
Confucius

Men are like steel.
When they lose their temper,
they lose their worth.
Chuck Norris

A black belt is a white belt that never quit.
(anonymous)

In the martial arts, introspection begets wisdom.
Always see contemplation on your actions
as an opportunity to improve.
Masutatsu Oyama

Chojun Miyagi Sensei refused to award dan grades
and the martial arts didn't have dan grades until
judo adopted them. I believe that there should be
black belts and white belts only, and that the focus
should be on training, not on accumulating rank.
Morio Higaonna

Mind and technique
become one in true karate.
Gichin Funakoshi

Live every moment with all your energy.
Don't stop, keep going, steadily. That is life.
Shigeru Uchiyama

The Paradox of Our Age

We have bigger houses, but smaller families;
more conveniences, but less time.

We have more degrees, but less sense,
more knowledge, but less judgment,
more experts, but more problems,
more medicines, but less healthiness.

We've been all the way to the moon and back,
but we have trouble crossing the street to meet the new
neighbor.

We built more computers to hold more information,
to produce more copies than ever, but have less
communication.

We have become long on quantity, but short on quality.
These are times of fast food, but slow digestion,
tall men, but short character,
steep profits, but shallow relationships.

It is a time when there is much in the window,
but nothing in the room.
~ *The Dalai Lama* ~

Karate is the best thing
you can do for your child.
Chuck Norris

A weapon isn't good or bad;
it depends on the person who uses it.
Jet Li

Cry in the dojo.
Laugh in the battlefield.
Japanese Proverb

The belt is just good for holding your pants up.
It is too thin to protect your ass from being kicked.
Helio Gracie

Don't think during practice – DO!
The more you think, the further
from the truth of budo you get.
Masaaki Hatsumi

Never quit.
You have to resist to the utmost.
Til you drop, like a samurai.
Carlson Gracie

If you want to break the ribs, punch with
the intent of thrusting your fist to the heart.
Masutatsu Oyama

Confidence comes from discipline and training.
Rubens Charles

Do not practice until you get it right.
Practice until you can't get it wrong.
Angela Minerva

The books that help you most are
those which make you think the most.
Theodore Parker

Any martial art, without the proper training
of the mind, becomes beastly behavior.
Shoshin Nagamine

The biggest gift I receive as a martial artist is,
without a question, the capacity to be in peace.
Rickson Gracie

In a real fight, there are no rules,
so we must learn to use weapons.
Masaaki Hatsumi

Act without expectations.
Lao Tzu

Do not be negligent, even in trivial matters.
Miyamoto Musashi

It is not the number of kata you know,
but the substance of the kata you have acquired.
Gogen Yamaguchi

Live being true to the
single purpose of the moment.
Yamamoto Tsunetomo

Love is the highest art. In ancient times you trained hard,
not for the sake of killing people, but for the love of your
family – for the love of your mother, your father, your
children, your tribe, and your body. It is the love of life.
That's why we train so hard, so you can preserve life.
Dan Inosanto

Don't fear failure.
Not failure, but low aim, is the crime.
In great attempts, it is glorious even to fail.
Bruce Lee

The ultimate aim of martial arts
is not having to use them.
Miyamoto Musashi

In the spirit of Zen and Budo, everyday life becomes the
contest. There must be awareness at every moment
getting up in the morning, eating, going to bed.
That is the place for self-mastery.
Taisen Deshimaru

If the spirit is strong, one will appear like a deep,
flowing river, calm on the surface, but with
tremendous power hidden in the depths.
Hideharu Onuma

Usually, a well thought out answer
makes an aggressor think twice.
Helio Gracie

If you meet a swordsman, draw your sword.
Do not recite poetry to one who is not a poet.
Buddhist Proverb

True Budo knows no defeat.
Winning means winning over
the mind of discord in yourself.
Morihei Ueshiba

Repetition is the mother of all skills.
Edgar Sulite

The approach to combat and
everyday life should be the same.
Miyamoto Musashi

Since Meiji times, foreign thoughts and culture, flowing
and entering in, have at last been changing sacred
Budo into sports, becoming competitive.
This situation is never true martial spirit.
Yoshio Sugino

The point in kata is to learn how to apply the
movements in reality, how to train the body
to adapt to situations in a flexible way.
Mitsusuke Harada

A martial artist always
takes responsibility for himself and
accepts the consequences of his own doing.
Bruce Lee

What you have been taught by listening
to others' words, you forget very quickly;
what you have learned with your whole body,
you will remember for the rest of your life.
Gichin Funakoshi

Pay your respects to the gods and Buddhas,
but never rely on them.
Miyamoto Musashi

The man who wishes to truly accomplish the way of Budo
must not train for skill and strength alone,
but also for spiritual attainment.
Masutatsu Oyama

As the spirit become like water and adapts to its
container, so you must adapt to your opponent.
Miyamoto Musashi

To reach me, you must move to me.
Your attack offers me an opportunity to intercept you.
Bruce Lee

A warrior is worthless unless he rises above others
and stands strong in the midst of a storm.
Yamamoto Tsunetomo

A man of peace, confident in himself,
dominates his adversary with his moral strength;
not with his physical power.
Helio Gracie

When two tigers fight,
one is certain to be maimed, and one to die.
Gichin Funakoshi

You can fight ten people and win now,
but eventually you will get old.
Eventually you can't fight anymore.
It is better to cultivate yourself and help
people use this art to improve their lives.
Wang Bo

The Man in the Arena

It is not the critic who counts, not the man who points out how the strong man stumbles, or where the doer of deeds could have done them better.

The credit belongs to the man in the arena, whose face is marred by dust and sweat and blood, who strives valiantly, who knows the great enthusiasms, the great devotions, who spends himself in a worthy cause, who at the best knows in the end the triumph of high achievement, and who at the worst, if he fails, at least fails while daring greatly, so that his place shall never be with those cold and timid souls who have never known neither victory nor defeat.

Theodore Roosevelt

What is the True Meaning of Life?

If Heaven is about to entrust an important mission to a man, it begins by filling his heart with bitterness and by confusing his powers of perception and overturning his plans. It forces him to exert his will and muscle. It forces him to endure hunger and all manner of sufferings. When the man emerges triumphantly over all these trials and tribulations, he is then capable of accomplishing what would have been impossible for him to do before.

Mencius

(This was the answer Mencius gave when asked, "What is the true meaning of life?")

The teaching of one virtuous person can influence many;
that which has been learned well by one generation
can be passed on to a hundred.
Jigoro Kano

If you think about real fighting, there are no rules.
So you better train every part of your body.
Bruce Lee

Wushu is a philosophy of life.
It is designed for defense, and not offense.
It is a way to bring your mind and body into focus.
Jet Li

It is difficult to understand the Universe
if you only study one planet.
Miyamoto Musashi

Remove yourself not just from the line of attack,
but from the line of your opponent's attention.
Vladimir Vasilier

Traditionalists often study what is taught,
not what there is to create.
Ed Parker

Calmness gives you an advantage when facing an
opponent. With it, you have much better instincts.
Lui Ming Fai

Become the master of the art, not its slave.
Wong Shun Leung

Paradoxically, the man who has failed and one who
is at the peak of success are in the same position.
Each must decide what to do next.
Jigoro Kano

I look around today and feel saddened. Many students
of martial arts do not have respect for their teachers.
All they want to learn is punching and kicking.
This is not martial arts, it is only fighting.
Hwang Kee

Understand that the essence of martial arts is not
the art itself, but what's hidden deep within yourself.
Gogen Yamaguchi

One or two out of every 100 students
reach black belt, and of those, only one
out of every 1,000 achieves his 2nd Dan.
Masutatsu Oyama

Change your style. It is easy to kill the bird on the wing
that flies straight; not that which turns. A gambler
does not play the card which his opponent
expects much less that which he desires.
Baltasar Gracian

Perceive that which cannot be seen with the eye.
Miyamoto Musashi

Master the divine techniques of the art of peace
and no enemy will dare to challenge you.
Morihei Ueshiba

Life is a succession of here and now,
here and now, unceasing concentration
in the here and now.
Taisen Deshimaru

The true meaning of Budo was lost.
I see a lot of people talking about training
in martial arts, however, when one looks closely
inside, there is no substance to what they are doing.
Sekiguchi Takaaki

Foster and polish the warrior spirit while serving in the
world; illuminate the path according to your inner light.
Morihei Ueshiba

A thousand days is just to forge the spirit.
Ten thousand days is to polish what you forged.
Miyamoto Musashi

Some warriors look fierce, but are mild.
Some seem timid, but are vicious.
Look beyond appearances;
position yourself for the advantage.
Deng Ming-Dao

As a Samurai, I must strengthen my character.
As a human being, I must perfect my spirit.
Yamaoka Tesshu

Karate is not about winning.
It's about not losing.
Shigetoshi Senaha

How you think when you lose,
determines how long it will be until you win.
G. K. Chesterton

The way of the martial arts is to make the heart
of the universe one's own heart, which simply
means making oneself one with the universe.
Morihei Ueshiba

Though few men can do it, it is very wise to hide
your displeasure with others, so long as it does you
no shame or harm. For it often happens that later you
will need the help of these people, and you can hardly
get it if they already know you dislike them.
Francesco Guicciardini

People will, in a great degree,
and not without reason,
form their opinion of you,
upon that which they have of your friends.
Lord Chesterfield

We should teach our children
with martial arts philosophy.
Jhoon Rhee

Iron is full of impurities that weaken it;
through forging, it becomes steel and can
be transformed into a razor-sharp sword.
Human beings develop in the same fashion.
Morihei Ueshiba

A tranquil man is tolerant.
There is no reason for me to beat
someone up if he calls me names.
This confidence is moral, not physical.
Helio Gracie

Only one person in a million becomes
enlightened without the help of a teacher.
Bodhidharma

Do not be tense; just be ready, not thinking but
not dreaming, not being set but being flexible.
It is being wholly and quietly alive, aware
and alert, ready for whatever may come.
Bruce Lee

If you develop a brave heart, dojo training
and a real fight have the same feeling.
Tatsuo Suzuki

If your enemies, who are usually united against you,
have started to fight among themselves, attacking
one of them in the hope of beating him separately
may well cause them to reunite.
Francesco Guicciardini

To practice Zen, or the martial arts, you must live
intensely, wholeheartedly, without reserve,
as if you might die in the next instant.
Taisen Deshinmaru

Karate is self-training in perfection.
It is training in efficiency.
It is training in self-defense.
It is training in self-reliance.
Shoshin Nagamine

You must be so good that you don't need to kill.
Imi Lichtenfeld

Wing Chun is not a game; it's for survival.
Samuel Kwok

If you are thinking that you are always
on the battlefield, you will be prepared.
Minoru Inaba

The difference between a real fight and
sparring on the mat is the difference between
swimming in the ocean and swimming in a pool.
Steven Seagal

Learning kung fu has only one purpose:
to train one's reaction into a natural response.
Such reaction is essential.
Yan Xiu Gang

To become the enemy,
see yourself as the enemy of the enemy.
Miyamoto Musashi

Fear is a great servant,
but a terrible master.
Kevin Blok

Every person that works with you is your instructor.
And those who want to beat you up
are your best instructors.
Mikhail Ryabko

The true science of martial arts means
practicing them in such a way that they
will be useful at any time, and to teach them
in such a way that they will be useful in all things.
Miyamoto Musashi

Don't get set into one form,
adapt it and build your own,
and let it grow. Be like water.
Bruce Lee

If you wish to control others,
you must first control yourself.
Miyamoto Musashi

The mystery existing between an open moment
and a person's preparedness reveals the truth.
Masatochi Nakayama

Your spirit is your true shield.
Morihei Ueshiba

Mental and spiritual disciplines are
very important aspects of the martial arts.
Hwang Kee

If today you have nothing to be happy about,
thank God for the potential of tomorrow.
Rickson Gracie

Your life is the true testament to your skill as
a martial artist, not your rank or your trophies.
Allen A. Abad

Training is not just for the physical, you have to train your
body, your mind, your brain and nervous system, your
inner energy, and your consciousness.
Hiro Watanabe

Ungovernable Temper

A Zen student came to Bankei and complained, "Master, I have an ungovernable temper. How can I cure it?"

"You have something very strange, said Bankei, "Please show it to me."

"I cannot show it to you at this moment," said the student.

"Well, when can you show it to me?" asked Bankei.

"It appears unexpectedly," replied the student.

"Then it must not be your true nature. If it were, you could show it to me at any time. It is something that you were not born with, but rather have allowed. It is not the true you."

Fight for Honor

He who fights for blood soon finds it dripping from his own heart. He who fights for glory never lives long enough to hear the victory songs. He who fights for gold is already blinded by the glitter and glare of his own greed, all too soon led astray by all things shiny. He who fights for sport seldom finds The Gods in a sporting mood. He who fights for love must leave the one he loves the most behind, so he can dance with the one he hates the most. But he who fights for honor cannot be led astray.
Hannibal

Kempo is for the street first;
everything else is secondary.
William Ah Sun Chow Hoon

The physical, mental and spiritual training of the
student should be combined as one. The heart,
mind, and body should be in union at all times.
Hohan Soken

The true value of Budo is to train the mind
to see clearly and maintain spiritual strength.
Takamatsu Toshitsugu

My opponent is my teacher;
my ego is my enemy.
Renzo Gracie

A single man can light the way for many.
Spartacus

One must master controlling oneself,
before being able to control the opponent.
Lui Ming Fai

Being natural is the
ultimate secret of our art.
Toshitsugu Takamatsu

The teacher, if indeed wise, does not bid you to
enter the house of their wisdom, but leads
you to the threshold of your own mind.
Kahil Gibran

The weakest always get it in the neck; for men do not act according to reason or consideration for others. Rather each seeks his own advantage, and all agree to make the weakest suffer because he is the one they least fear.
Francesco Guicciardini

Don't show pain.
Your opponent will see it.
Masutatsu Oyama

I'll give you the answer to the question:
What is most important to the heart of a warrior?
The answer is to desire with one's very soul, every second of every day, to accomplish one's aim.
Yamamotoa Tsunetomo

When the victory is yours,
tighten your helmet cords.
Japanese Proverb

Philosophy is most important in learning ninjutsu.
Just teaching technique is wrong.
If someone is only teaching technique,
he is not an ninja.
Masaaki Hatsumi

A sound offense has the power of roaring water,
it fills every hole in an opponent's defenses.
Choi Hong Hi

Wherever you go, go with all your heart.
Confucius

When you have more confidence in yourself,
you become automatically more tolerant.
Helio Gracie

The way of the warrior has been misunderstood.
It is not a means to kill and destroy others.
Those who seek to compete and better one
another are making a terrible mistake.
To smash, injure, or destroy is the
worst thing a human being can do.
The real way of a warrior is to prevent such slaughter.
Morihei Ueshiba

When you discard your expectations of what
you think Budo is, patience begins its work.
Masaaki Hatsumi

Every opponent has a strategy. Your ultimate purpose
is to cancel this strategy before he enforces it on you.
Constantinos Glavas

Shuchu Ryoku – Focus all your energy to one point.
Gozo Shioda

Simply act decisively with reserve!
Morehei Ueshiba

Winning is not a sometime thing; it's an all time thing.
You don't win once in a while, you don't do things right
once in a while, you do them right all the time.
Winning is a habit. Unfortunately, so is losing.
Vince Lombardi

Vibrant and intense living is the warrior's form of worship.
Stephen K. Hayes

Spirit first, technique second.
Gichin Funakoshi

Pain is the best instructor,
but no one wants to go to his class.
Hong Hi Choi

Live your life so that when you die,
the world cries and you rejoice.
Cherokee Maxim

Talent develops in tranquility,
character in the full current of human life.
Goethe

He who has a "why" to live for can bear almost any how.
Friedrich Nietzsche

When, in a split second, your life is threatened, do you say,
"Let me make sure my hand is on my hip, and my style
is the style?" When your life is in danger, do you
argue about the method you will adhere to
while saving yourself? Why the duality?
Bruce Lee

In a fight between a strong technique
and a strong body, technique will prevail.
In a fight between a strong mind and a strong technique,
mind will prevail, because it will find the weak point.
Taisen Deshimaru

So long as there is breath in me, that long will I persist.
For now I know one of the greatest principles of success;
if I persists long enough, I will win.
Og Mandino

Far better it is to dare mighty things, to win
glorious triumphs even though checkered by failure,
than to rank with those poor spirits who neither enjoy
nor suffer much because they live in the gray twilight
that knows neither victory nor defeat.
Theodore Roosevelt

Courage is being to death
but saddling up anyway.
John Wayne

Silence is the safest policy
if you are unsure of yourself.
La Rochefoucauld

Courage, above all things,
is the first quality of a warrior.
Karl Von Clausewitz

It's not the size of the dog in the fight,
it's the size of the fight in the dog.
Mark Twain

If I do my full duty,
the rest will take care of itself.
George S. Patton

Whether one moves or remains still,
the body remains constantly at peace.
Even if one finds oneself facing a sword,
the mind remains tranquil.
Shodoka

In a moment of decision, the best
thing you can do is the right thing to do.
The worst thing you can do is nothing.
Theodore Roosevelt

Failure is the key to success;
each mistake teaches us something.
Morihei Ueshiba

Excellence is an art won by training and habit.
We do not act rightly because we have
virtue or excellence, but we have those
because we have acted rightly.
We are what we repeatedly do.
Excellence, then, is not an act, but a habit.
Aristotle

Words rule the world. So rule your words.
Sword and spear wound. Words, even more so.
Spartacus

The winners in life think constantly
in terms of I can, I will, and I am.
Losers, on the other hand, concentrate
their waking thoughts on what they should
have or would have done, or what they can't do.
Dennis Waitly

Now and again, it is necessary to seclude yourself
among deep mountains and hidden valleys
to restore your link to the source of life.
Morehei Ueshiba

Truth is universal.
Perception of truth varies.
Bohdi Sanders

My forefathers were warriors.
Their son is a warrior.
I am the maker of my own fortune.
Tecumseh

The fire of anger only burns the angry.
Chinese Proverb

To generate great power you must first totally relax
and gather your strength, and then concentrate your
mind and all your strength on hitting your target.
Bruce Lee

Never be misled by what your foe does.
If a fool, he will not do what a wiser man
thinks best, because he never knows what
is best; and if a man of discretion, not then,
because he wishes to cloak his intent.
Baltasar Gracian

A natural mind is most important. If you try to speak
without this state of mind, you voice will tremble.
Yagyu Tajimanokami Munenori

To know something means
having experienced it concretely.
A cookbook will not take away your hunger.
Takuan Soho

IF

If you can keep your head when all about you
Are losing theirs and blaming it on you;
If you can trust yourself when all men doubt you,
But make allowance for their doubting too;

If you can wait and not be tired by waiting,
Or, being lied about, don't deal in lies,
Or, being hated, don't give way to hating,
And yet don't look too good, nor talk too wise;

If you can dream - and not make dreams your master;
If you can think - and not make thoughts your aim;
If you can meet with triumph and disaster
And treat those two impostors just the same;

If you can bear to hear the truth you've spoken
Twisted by knaves to make a trap for fools,
Or watch the things you gave your life to broken,
And stoop and build 'em up with worn-out tools;

If you can make one heap of all your winnings
And risk it on one turn of pitch-and-toss,
And lose, and start again at your beginnings
And never breathe a word about your loss;

If you can force your heart and nerve and sinew
To serve your turn long after they are gone,
And so hold on when there is nothing in you
Except the Will which says to them: "Hold on!"

If you can talk with crowds and keep your virtue,
Or walk with kings - nor lose the common touch;
If neither foes nor loving friends can hurt you;
If all men count with you, but none too much;

If you can fill the unforgiving minute
With sixty seconds' worth of distance run -
Yours is the Earth and everything that's in it,
And - which is more - you'll be a Man, my son!

Rudyard Kipling

In cases of defense tis best to weigh
the enemy more mighty than he seems.
William Shakespeare

Be careful that your enemy
doesn't catch you napping.
Matsura Seizan

There are few men in the world who love, and at the same
time, know the bad qualities of the one that they love. Or
who hate, and yet see the goodness of the one they hate.
The Ta Hsueh

Mind, not only what people say,
but how they say it.
Lord Chesterfield

If you practice martial arts without kokoro,
you will find that you are out of balance. You must
put your spirit, mind and heart into everything you do.
Bohdi Sanders

Our greatest source of power is not at the end of our hands
and feet. Our greatest source of power comes from within.
Once we are able to tap into this internal source of
energy, only then will we will recognize our true potential.
Robert Cutrell

Training is not just for the physical, you have to train your
body, your mind, your brain and your nervous system,
your inner energy, and your consciousness.
Hiro Watanabe

Nothing is more harmful to the world than a martial art
that is not effective in actual self-defense.
Choki Motobu

All you learn, and all you can read, will be of little use,
if you do not think and reason upon it yourself.
Lord Chesterfield

To the ignorant, a precious stone
looks like a simple pebble.
Japanese Proverb

An ordinary man will draw his sword if he feels that he
has been ridiculed, and risk his very life, but he will not
be called a courageous man for doing so. A superior man
is never alarmed, even in the most unexpected situations,
because he has a great soul and noble objective."
Gichin Funakoshi

Do not regret what you have done.
Miyamoto Musashi

The heights by great men
reached and kept
were not attained
by sudden flight.
But they, while their
companions slept,
were toiling upward
in the night.
Henry Wadsworth Longfellow

Street fights are unpredictable, dirty fights.
Imi Lichtenfeld

A wise man, in great or small matters,
must act with due consideration.
Whether attacking a hare or an elephant,
the lion has no time for indecision.
Sakya Pandit

I realized that perseverance and step-by-step progress
are the only ways to reach a goal along a chosen path.
Masutatsu Oyama

A good teacher can never be fixed in a routine.
Each movement requires a sensitive mind that is
constantly changing and constantly adapting.
Bruce Lee

Words always cost more than silence.
Vlad Tepes

Take what you have and think of
a way to improve or simplify it.
Ted Wong

Double the fear in your enemy's heart and you halve
the chance he'll ever put a sword in his hand.
Vlad Tepes

Knowing when to walk away,
is WISDOM.
Being able to walk away,
is COURAGE.
Walking away with your head held high,
is DIGNITY.
(anonymous)

What a man loves, what he hates,
what he needs, what he desires:
These are the four pillars that support his house.
Hannibal

The weakest foe boasts some revenging powers.
Benjamin Franklin

Where the hawk cannot strike down the great bear,
he can surely blind him with a well-placed talon!
Vlad Tepes

If the enemy is in range, so are you.
Murphy's Laws of Combat

Simplicity is the key to brilliance.
Bruce Lee

There is nothing impossible to him who will try.
Alexander the Great

Running away is the first of wisdoms.
Turning suddenly, the first of strategies.
Spartacus

Train more than you sleep.
Masutatsu Oyama

The power of the mind in infinite,
while brawn is limited.
Koichi Tohei

Never fight empty-handed unless you're forced to.
Kelly McCann

Cultivate the root.
Confucius

In war, there is no substitute for victory.
General Douglas MacArthur

We can fight the sword or we can
fight the man swinging the sword.
Which one breaks more easily?
Break your enemy's sword, and
he will soon purchase another.
Break his courage, and what
merchant sells that keenest of blades?
Spartacus

When the cat and the rat hunt cheese together, the rat
practices wishful thinking while the cat practices patience.
Vlad Tepes

Expect anything from anyone.
The devil was once an angel.
Drake Graham

I am not afraid of an army of lions led by a sheep;
I am afraid of an army of sheep led by a lion.
Alexander the Great

Like a sword, a word can wound or kill...
Someone who knows the qualities of a sword,
does not play with it, and someone who knows
the nature of words, do not play with them.
Miyamoto Musashi

We must first set our hearts right.
Confucius

You cannot be disciplined in great things
and undisciplined in small things.
General George S. Patton

You have no enemies, you say?
Alas, my friend, the boast is poor.
He who has mingled in the fray of
duty, that the brave endure, must
have made foes! If you have none,
small is the work you have done.
You've hit no traitor on the hip.
You've dashed no cup from perjured lip.
You've never turned the wrong to right.
You've been a coward in the fight.
Charles MacKay

I learned that good judgment comes from experience
and that experience grows out of mistakes.
General Omar N. Bradley

Notice that the stiffest tree is most easily cracked, while
the bamboo or willow survives by bending with the wind.
Bruce Lee

Cowards die many times before their deaths,
the valiant never taste of death but once.
Shakespeare

Human beings,
by changing the inner attitudes of their minds,
can change the outer aspects of their lives.
William James

The price of freedom is eternal vigilance.
Thomas Jefferson

Never respond to an angry person with
a fiery comeback, even if he deserves it.
Don't allow his anger to become your anger.
Bohdi Sanders

You can only fight the way you practice.
Miyamoto Musashi

I Choose...
To live by choice, not chance.
To make changes, not excuses.
To be motivated, not manipulated.
To be useful, not used.
To excel, not compete.
I choose self-esteem, not pity.
To listen to my inner voice, and
not the random opinions of others.
(anonymous)

Be Water, My Friend

Be like water making its way through cracks.
Do not be assertive, but adjust to the object,
and you shall find a way around or through it.
If nothing within you stays rigid, outward
Things will disclose themselves.

Empty your mind, be formless.
Shapeless, like water.
If you put water into a cup, it becomes the cup.
You put water into a bottle and it becomes the bottle.
You put it in a teapot, it becomes the teapot.
Now, water can flow or it can crash.
Be water, my friend.
Bruce Lee

Index

About the Author

Dr. Bohdi Sanders is a multi-award winning author and 6-time Martial Arts Hall of Fame inductee. His previous book, *Modern Bushido*, hit #1 on Amazon and has been in the TOP 10 for a total of 90 weeks. Dr. Sanders has been awarded the title of Hanshi and the rank of 10th Dan Black Belt. He also serves on the board of The Extreme Budo Federation, along with several other esteemed martial artists.

Dr. Sanders is also a Certified Personal Fitness Trainer, a Certified Specialist in Martial Arts Conditioning, a Certified Reiki Master, and a Certified Master of G-Jo Acupressure. He holds a black belt in Shotokan Karate and has studied various other martial arts for over 30 years. He is the author of:

- *Modern Bushido: Living a Life of Excellence*
- *Warrior Wisdom: Ageless Wisdom for the Modern Warrior*
- *Warrior: The Way of Warriorhood*
- *The Warrior Lifestyle: Making Your Life Extraordinary*
- *Defensive Living: The Other Side of Self-Defense*
- *Wisdom of the Elders: The Ultimate Quote Book for Life*
- *Secrets of the Soul, and more.*

Dr. Sanders' books have received high praise and have won several national awards, including:

- U. S. Martial Arts Hall of Fame: Warrior Award 2013
- #1 on Amazon.com's Best Seller List: *Modern Bushido* 2013
- The Indie Excellence Book Awards: 1st Place Winner 2013
- USA Book News Best Books of 2013: 1st Place Winner 2013
- IIMAA Best Martial Arts Book of the Year 2011
- U. S. Martial Arts Hall of Fame: Author of the Year 2011
- U. S. Martial Artist Association: Inspiration of the Year 2011
- USA Martial Arts HOF: Literary Man of the Year 2011
- The Indie Excellence Book Awards: 1st Place Winner 2010
- USA Book News Best Books of 2010: 1st Place Winner 2010

Other Titles by Bohdi Sanders

Character! Honor! Integrity! Are these traits that guide your life and actions? *Warrior Wisdom: Ageless Wisdom for the Modern Warrior* focuses on how to live your life with character, honor and integrity. *Warrior Wisdom* reached #5 on Amazon.com and has won multiple awards and is endorsed by some of the biggest names in martial arts. *Warrior Wisdom* is filled with wise quotes and useful information for anyone who strives to live a life of excellence. This book will help you live your life to the fullest.

Warrior: The Way of Warriorhood is the second book in the *Warrior Wisdom Series*. Wisdom, life-changing quotes, and entertaining, practical commentaries fill every page. This series has been recognized by four martial arts hall of fame organizations for its inspirational and motivational qualities. The ancient and modern wisdom in this book will definitely help you improve your life and bring meaning to each and every day. The USMAA Hall of Fame awarded Dr. Sanders with Inspiration of the Year for this series!

The Warrior Lifestyle is the last installment of the award winning *Warrior Wisdom Series*. Reaching the TOP 10 on Amazon.com, this book has been dubbed as highly inspirational and motivational. If you want to live your life to the fullest, you need to read this one! Don't settle for an ordinary life, make your life extraordinary! The advice and wisdom shines on every page of this book, making it a must read for everyone who strives to live an extraordinary life of character and honor!

Other Titles by Bohdi Sanders

Wisdom of the Elders is a unique, one-of-a-kind quote book. This book is filled with quotes that focus on living life to the fullest with honor, character, and integrity. Honored by the USA Book News with a 1st place award for Best Books of the Year in 2010, this book is a guide for life. *Wisdom of the Elders* contains over 4,800 quotes, all which lead the reader to a life of excellence. If you enjoy quotes, wisdom, and knowledge, you will love this book. This is truly the ultimate quote book for those searching for wisdom!

Defensive Living takes the reader deep into the minds of nine of the most revered masters of worldly wisdom. It reveals valuable insights concerning human nature from some of the greatest minds the world has ever known, such as Sun Tzu, Gracian, Goethe, and others. *Defensive Living* presents invaluable lessons for living, and advice for avoiding the many pitfalls of human relationships. This is an invaluable and entertaining guidebook for living a successful and rewarding life!

Modern Bushido is the award-winning bestseller that hit #1 on Amazon.com! Honored by the USA Martial Arts Hall of Fame, this book covers 30 essential traits that will change your life. *Modern Bushido* expands on the principles needed for a life of excellence, and applies them directly to life in today's world. Readers will be motivated and inspired by the straightforward wisdom in this enlightening book. This is a must read for everyone who wants to live a life of character, honor, and integrity!

Honors for Dr. Sanders' Books

Dr. Sanders' books have been honored by the follow organizations for their significant contributions to the world of martial arts:

- U. S. Martial Arts Hall of Fame:
  Warrior Award 2013 – *Modern Bushido*
- #1 on Amazon.com's Best Seller List:
  Martial Arts Books – *Modern Bushido*
- The Indie Excellence Book Awards:
  1st Place Winner 2013 – *Modern Bushido*
- USA Book News Best Books of 2013:
  1st Place Winner 2013 – *Modern Bushido*
- International Independent Martial Arts Assoc.:
  Best Martial Arts Book of the Year 2011
- U. S. Martial Arts Hall of Fame:
  Author of the Year 2011
- U. S. Martial Artist Association:
  Inspiration of the Year 2011
- USA Martial Arts HOF:
  Literary Man of the Year 2011
- The Indie Excellence Book Awards:
  1st Place Winner 2010 – *Warrior Wisdom*
- USA Book News Best Books of 2010:
  1st Place Winner 2010 – *Wisdom of the Elders*

Looking for More Wisdom?

If you are interested in living the warrior lifestyle or simply in living a life of character, integrity and honor you will enjoy The Wisdom Warrior website and newsletter. The Wisdom Warrior website contains dozens of articles, useful links, and news for those seeking to live the warrior lifestyle.

The newsletter is also a valuable resource. Each edition of The Wisdom Warrior Newsletter is packed with motivating quotes, articles, and information which everyone will find useful in their journey to perfect their character and live the life which they were meant to live.

The Wisdom Warrior Newsletter is a newsletter sent directly to your email account and is absolutely FREE! There is no cost or obligation to you whatsoever. You will also receive the current news updates and new articles by Dr. Bohdi Sanders as soon as they are available.

All you need to do to start receiving this valuable and informative newsletter is to go to the Wisdom Warrior website and simply sign up. It is that simple! You will find The Wisdom Warrior website at:

www.TheWisdomWarrior.com

Also, be sure to find posts by Dr. Sanders on Facebook. Dr. Sanders posts enlightening commentaries, photographs, and quotes throughout the week on his Facebook pages. You can find them at:

www.Facebook.com/The.Warrior.Lifestyle

www.Google.com/+BohdiSanders

www.Twitter.com/BohdiSanders

Don't miss the opportunity to receive tons of FREE wisdom, enlightening posts, interesting articles, and intriguing photographs on The Wisdom Warrior website and on Dr. Sanders' Facebook pages.

Sign Up Today!

37841652R00089

Made in the USA
Lexington, KY
15 December 2014